Dickens' London

Pentonville

ock
home
60

Doughty Street - Dickens' home 1837-39

Dials -
nt of criminal
n Dickens' time.

Holborn

Chancery Lane

y Lane

vent
rden

Strand

Fleet Prison (Pickwick was held here)

Newgate Prison (Fagin was held here before his execution)

City Road

Bishopsgate

Guild hall - Dickens slept here as a lost boy

The City

Whitechapel

Somerset House - John Dickens worked here

Blackfriars Bridge

George and Vulture Inn (Pickwick stayed here.)

en's
cking
ry

Scotland Yard - Inspector Field worked here

Waterloo Bridge

Waterloo Bridge

Great Surrey Street

Southwark Bridge

London Bridge (Nancy met Mr Brownlow here)

Bridge Street

Borough High Street

THAMES

estminster (David Copperfield crossed old Westminster Bridge)

Bridge

King's Bench Prison (Mr Micawber was held here.)

Borough Road

The Marshalsea - John Dickens was held here

Jacob's Island (Bill Sikes was chased across the rooftops here.)

Charles Dickens

SCENES FROM AN EXTRAORDINARY LIFE

For the inimitable Elizona Home Robertson

1938 - 2010

JANETTA OTTER-BARRY BOOKS

Charles Dickens was born on 7th February, 1812. He became one of the greatest writers who ever lived. Yet he never wrote down his own life story. In fact he kept details of his childhood secret for many years. Eventually he did talk, revealing that many of his characters and exciting stories, especially *David Copperfield*, were based on events in his own life.

By respectfully borrowing from his own words: conversations, letters, quotes and writings, as well as his own children's fond recollections, Mick and Brita have invited Mr Dickens to show you some of the scenes from his extraordinary life.

Charles Dickens

SCENES FROM AN EXTRAORDINARY LIFE

Mick Manning & Brita Granström

F

FRANCES LINCOLN
CHILDREN'S BOOKS

Charles Dickens was born into an age of war and revolution. . .

when war against France still raged, the Prince Regent ruled and the future Queen Victoria hadn't even been born.

No jobs for us here any more.

In the early 1800s Britain was in a state of change. . . The inventions of the Agricultural Revolution meant machines now did the work of many farm labourers. Thousands lost their jobs – and the homes that went with them.

I have to crawl under the machine to clean it.

My mate lost a finger last week!

I'm only 7 years old and I have to sweep chimneys.

Thousands of families crowded into towns, working in the mills, mines and factories of the Industrial Revolution. Child workers did many dangerous jobs while others were forced, by hunger and poverty, into crime. These were the people Charles Dickens would one day feel such sympathy for and write about.

We shall call him Charles... What do you think, Fanny?

Charles is a nice name, Father.

John Dickens was a wages clerk for the Royal Navy. This job moved him and his family from place to place around the shipyards near London. Elizabeth Dickens had a talent for comic voices and taught her son to read at an early age.

BABY DICKENS – 1812
In which Charles Dickens is born in Portsmouth, England

I was born on a Friday, at twelve o'clock at night. It was remarked that the clock began to strike, and I began to cry, simultaneously. Whether I shall turn out to be the hero of my own life these pages must show. . .

In 1817 John Dickens was posted to work as a pay clerk at Chatham Docks. Sometimes he would take Charles and his sister Fanny with him around the noisy shipyard, and even sail past the old prison hulks.

HAPPY DAYS – 1821
In which young Charles first performs in public

In Chatham I told a story so well and sang small comic songs so especially well, that I used to be lifted by my father on to the chairs and tables of local inns to display these talents. I blush to think now, what a horrible little nuisance I must have been to many grown-ups who were called upon to admire me!

Well done, my boy, well done!

Rule Britannia Britannia rules the waves!

The Dickens family lived next to a small theatre in Sheerness for a while. Songs came thumping through the thin wall – and the whole family would often join in!

Work hard, my boy – and you might afford such a house one day!

Dickens and his father sometimes walked past Gad's Hill Place. Many years later, in 1856, Dickens returned and bought that very same house.

MOVING TO LONDON – 1822
In which the Dickens family move to Camden Town

I left in a stagecoach. Through all the years that have since passed, have I ever lost the smell of damp straw in which I was packed – like game – and forwarded, carriage paid, to London? There was no other inside passenger, and I consumed my sandwiches in solitude and dreariness, and it rained hard all the way, and I thought life sloppier than I expected to find it.

When his family moved to London, Charles finished the term at his old school. But school wasn't free in those days and John Dickens couldn't afford to continue Charles's education. So Charles stayed at home, reading books such as *Robinson Crusoe*.

I'm a very small and not-over-particularly-taken-care-of boy...

What a noisy, smelly place!

This is your new home, Charlie-boy! London town!

An early tragedy for Charles was the death of his little sister, Harriet, in 1824. She died of smallpox – a common disease in those days.

LOST! – 1823
In which 11-year-old Charles gets lost on the London streets – and then goes exploring

When I was a very small boy indeed both in years and in stature, I got lost one day in London… the child's terror of being lost comes as fresh on me now as it did then. I cried a little but soon made up my mind to go and see the Giants in Guildhall. I came into their presence at last and gazed up at them with dread… they were very big… Being very tired, I got into the corner and fell asleep. When I started up after a nap I thought the giants were roaring, but it was only the city.

When young Dickens got lost he must have seen many characters to remember, including pickpockets and rogues, in the bustling streets.

London's population exploded during the 1800s. London was filthy; sewage polluted drinking water, and the rivers became open sewers. Epidemics killed thousands of people every year.

Theatres were the cheap entertainment of the day, packed with all kinds of people. Charles had a toy theatre, and from an early age he wrote and even acted in some of his own plays.

'Hearts of oak are our ships,
Jolly tars are our men,
We always are ready,
Steady, boys, steady.'

Rule, Britannia.

Hee-haw!

Boo!

Sing!

ALONE! – 1823
In which Charles visits a theatre... all on his own

I had my sixpence clutched in my hand ready to pay; and when the doors opened, with a clattering of bolts, I went on with the current like a straw. When I came to the back of the gallery the seats looked so horribly steep. However a good-natured baker with a young woman gave me his hand, and we all three scrambled over the seats into the corner of the first row. The baker was very fond of the young woman and kissed her a good deal in the course of the evening.

Charles didn't stay lost. A kindly night-watchman looked after him until his father collected him.

No more credit, Sir!

John Dickens had been borrowing money he could not pay back. He owed money to many people, including the butcher and baker.

These bills must be paid, dear!

Charles must go to work!

In later years Charles once said that John, his father, had 'no money sense'.

He can come and work for me!

When a relative proposed that Charles should work for him for six shillings a week, the offer was gladly accepted by his father and mother.

I MUST WORK! – 1824
In which 12-year-old Charles is forced by his parents to get a job

Warren's Blacking Warehouse was a crazy, tumbledown old house, on the river and overrun with old grey rats. My work was to cover the pots of paste-blacking and to tie them round with a string. I was to paste on each a printed label; and then go on again with more pots. Two or three other boys were on similar wages. One of them came up to show me the trick of using the string and tying the knot. His name was Bob Fagin… No words can express the secret agony of my soul! My whole nature was so penetrated with grief and humiliation.

Let's have some fun with that new kid, Bill.
He speaks posh! I'm going to thump him.
I'm Bob Fagin. Who are you?
How can I be so easily cast away at such an age?

Goodness me!

The punishment for owing money in those days was a debtors' prison such as the Marshalsea. But once inside, you couldn't work – so how could you pay off your debts?

Elizabeth sold everything of value to pay their rent and buy food. Charles even had to sell beloved books such as: _Tales from the Arabian Nights_, _Tom Jones_ and _Robinson Crusoe_.

MY FATHER IS ARRESTED! – 1824
In which Charles's father is sent to the Marshalsea debtors' prison

I know that we got on very badly with the butcher and baker; that very often we had not too much for dinner and that at last my father was arrested…. In the debtors' prison, my father was waiting for me… we went up to his room and cried very much. And he told me, I remember, to take warning by the Marshalsea…. I see the fire we sat before now: with two bricks inside the rusted grate, one on each side, to prevent its burning too many coals.

Eventually, unable to pay the rent, the whole family moved into the prison with John – apart from Charles. At 12 years old, he had to take lodgings near his job.

I really believe they have broken my heart.

Annual income twenty pounds, annual expenditure nineteen pounds, nineteen and six, result happiness! Annual income twenty pounds, annual expenditure twenty pounds and six, result misery!

Charles must go back to school, Elizabeth!

Eventually John Dickens paid his debtors with a small inheritance from his mother. But Elizabeth disagreed about their son going back to school. Charles never forgave his mother for wanting him to stay at the factory.

SCHOOL AT LAST! – 1825
In which his father is freed and Charles can at last go to school again

At last, my father said I should go back no more, and should go to school: but I never afterwards forgot, I never shall forget, I never can forget, that my mother was for me being sent back.

Our school was remarkable for white mice. Linnets, and even canaries, were kept in desks, drawers, hat-boxes, and other strange refuges; but white mice were the favourites. The boys trained the mice much better than the masters trained the boys.

Because of his father's money troubles, Charles left school for good in 1827 and became a lawyer's office boy. In his spare time he and a fellow clerk would perform at a local theatre. In 1828, Dickens left the office to work as a newspaper reporter.

Charles began to write short stories too, and *A Dinner at Poplar Walk* was published in the Old Strand Magazine in 1833. His stories began to be published so regularly that Dickens invented a pen-name for himself, 'Boz' (pronounced 'Bowz').

I AM A REPORTER – 1827-33
In which Charles is first employed as an office-boy, then becomes a reporter at the age of 16

I have often transcribed important public speeches on the palm of my hand, by the light of a dark lantern, in a post-chaise and four, galloping through wild country, through the dead of the night!
I have had to charge for the damage of a greatcoat from the drippings of a blazing wax-candle, in writing through the smallest hours of the night in a swift-flying carriage and pair. I have had to charge for all sorts of breakages. I have charged for broken hats, broken luggage, broken chaises, broken harness – everything but a broken head.

Dickens was shocked to hear from his publishers, Chapman and Hall, that his father, again in debt, had been sending them begging letters.

LOVE AND MARRIAGE – 1835-37
In which our hero gets married, moves into Doughty Street and publishes *The Pickwick Papers*

I could now afford a pleasant, twelve-room dwelling of pink brick, with three stories and an attic, an arched entrance door and a small private garden in the rear. It was located just north of Gray's Inn… a genteel, private street with a lodge at each end and gates that were closed at night by a porter in a gold-laced hat and a mulberry-coloured coat…

THE PICKWICK PAPERS (1836-37) was published in monthly parts. The full-figured **Mr Pickwick** soon became famous and made Dickens' name as a young author.

Mr Pickwick and his friends form a club and have many adventures – and misadventures. . .

The stories are full of slapstick humour, comic mishaps and even a duel.

Mr Pickwick's servant, the cockney comedian, Sam Weller, made his readers hoot with laughter and turned the serial into a huge success.

Dickens began to write articles for the Evening Chronicle, becoming a friend of the editor George Hogarth and his daughters: Catherine, Mary and Georgina.

Charles married Catherine in 1836 and they moved into 48 Doughty Street the same year. This is now the home of The Dickens House Museum.

The last words she whispered were of me...

Dear Charles...

Dickens' beloved sister-in-law, Mary, died suddenly at Doughty Street in 1837. He was heartbroken and later wrote: 'So young and beautiful. She died in my arms.'

If I can just get the character of Bill Sikes!

OLIVER! – 1837
In which Dickens, at 25 years of age, writes a new serial for a magazine called *Bentley's Miscellany*

I wrote busily and rapidly at my desk, suddenly jumping up from my chair and rushing to a mirror in which I could see the reflection of some extraordinary facial contortions I was making. I then returned to my desk, wrote furiously for a few moments. . . and then my facial pantomime was resumed. I also began talking rapidly in a low voice. I threw myself completely into the character that I was creating; I had not only lost sight of my surroundings, but had actually become in action, as in imagination, the creature of my pen.

OLIVER TWIST (1837-38) is a story of the workhouse and criminal gangs.

A poor orphan boy, Oliver Twist, is brought up in a workhouse run by Mr Bumble, a cruel (but also comic) figure of authority.

The children are starving and draw lots to ask for food.

Oliver loses and has to ask for more gruel – a sticky sort of porridge.

He is beaten and eventually sold for five pounds as an apprentice to a gloomy undertaker.

When bullied by an older apprentice, he fights back and runs away.

All alone, Oliver makes his way to London.

He meets a young pickpocket called 'The Artful Dodger'.

Dodger takes Oliver to his gang leader, a mysterious old thief called Fagin.

Later, Dodger and another lad pick the pocket of a man called Mr Brownlow. Oliver is with them and gets the blame.

A terrifying judge called Mr Fang wants to punish Oliver.

Luckily the bookseller proves Oliver innocent, and Mr Brownlow takes care of him.

Scared that Oliver will betray their hide-out, Fagin sends a teenage girl, Nancy, along with a violent criminal called Bill Sikes, to kidnap Oliver and bring him back.

Oliver is forced to help burgle a house... but the robbery goes wrong. Oliver is shot and left for dead.

At the house a young woman called Rose nurses him back to health.

Sikes is chased across the roof-tops by the police and falls to his death, tangled in ropes.

Fagin is arrested and later hanged... But what happens to Oliver? Read the story yourself to find out!

Hablot Knight Browne had illustrated Dickens' stories since *The Pickwick Papers*, inventing his own nickname 'Phiz' to match 'Boz'. They were firm friends.

SMIKE! – 1838
In which our hero visits a dreadful school and writes *Nicholas Nickleby*

Depend upon it! The rascalities of those Yorkshire schoolmasters cannot easily be exaggerated. There is an old church near the school, and the first grave-stone I stumbled on was the grave of a boy who had died at that wretched place. I think his ghost put Smike into my head…

Dickens and 'Phiz' travelled to Yorkshire to visit one of the infamous 'Yorkshire schools', to which unwanted boys were sent and treated very badly. Its owner, William Shaw, shared the initials of, and became the model for, Wackford Squeers.

NICHOLAS NICKLEBY (1838-39) caused a public outcry, forcing many 'Yorkshire Schools' to close forever.

Nicholas's father dies, leaving him and his sister Kate penniless. Uncle Ralph, a ruthless businessman, takes charge of their lives.

He sends Nicholas away to teach at a 'Yorkshire School'. Dotheboy's Hall (do-the-boys) is a place for unwanted boys run by the Squeers family.

Wackford Squeers delights in hurting the boys, and encourages 'young Wackford' to be a bully too.

Nicholas befriends a poor boy called Smike who is treated like a slave and beaten.

Nicholas defends Smike, giving Squeers a taste of his own medicine by beating him in a fight…

Nicholas and Smike run away together and join a troupe of travelling actors. Happy days follow, for both of them. But meanwhile…

his sister, Kate, is being used by his uncle as a play-thing for his rich clients.

Nicholas returns to London. A chance meeting with the kind Cheeryble brothers gives him a good job. Next, he falls in love with Madeline, the penniless daughter of a debtor. He also rescues Kate by breaking all contact with his uncle Ralph. Kate falls in love with the Cheerybles' nephew, Frank. A happy ending?

We discover that Smike was actually Uncle Ralph's long-lost son, making Nicholas and Smike cousins. Sadly, Smike is also secretly in love with Kate. But he catches tuberculosis – a fatal illness in those days…

Smike dies, confessing his love for Kate with his last breath. Nicholas marries Madeline, Kate marries Frank… What a story!

SAILING FOR AMERICA – 1842
In which the now-famous Mr Dickens sets sail for the USA

Picture the sky both dark and wild, and the clouds making another ocean in the air. Add to all this, the clattering on deck; the tread of hurried feet; the loud, hoarse shouts of seamen; the gurgling in and out of water through the scuppers; with, every now and then, the striking of a heavy sea upon the planks above. If Neptune himself had walked in with a toasted shark on his trident, I should have looked upon the event as one of the very commonest everyday occurrences.

When Charles and Catherine visited the United States aboard the paddle steamship, *Britannia*, they found crowds waiting on the quayside, begging for news of Little Nell.

THE OLD CURIOSITY SHOP (1840 – 41) had first been serialised in Dickens' own magazine, *Master Humphrey's Clock*.

I've lost again.

I'll lend you money!

Come on, Grandfather...

Do you know where she is?

Nell Trent, a clever and sweet-natured, 13-year-old orphan girl runs a 'curiosity shop' (a sort of antiques shop) with her grandfather.

But Grandfather gambles all his money away on cards...

He borrows money from an evil man called Quilp.

Quilp evicts them from their shop and they become poor, wandering beggars.

Nell is hunted by her brother and his friend, Dick, because Quilp lets them think she is rich!

When the last, sad episode was published it made grown men cry.

Parted from their children for six months, Charles and Catherine took a family portrait with them as a keepsake.

President John Tyler invited Dickens to The White House and Dickens thought him 'gentlemanly, and agreeable'.

Dickens also met the Native American, Peter Pitchlynn, known as 'Snapping Turtle', who later became president of the Choctaw nation, campaigning for the return of tribal land. He sent Dickens his portrait.

AMERICA! – 1842
In which the American fans treat Dickens like a true superstar

I can't tell you what they do here to welcome me. Or how they cheer and shout… I can do nothing that I want to do, go nowhere where I want to go, and see nothing that I want to see. If I turn into the street, I am followed by a multitude.

When Dickens visited the New York slums, the haunt of criminal gangs, he had to be guarded by the police.

Visiting Niagara Falls, Dickens felt the ground tremble under his feet.

Dickens wrote many episodes of his stories while on holiday in Broadstairs, a seaside holiday resort in Kent.

I will just finish this chapter...

Good heavens, young man! Men are not supposed to bathe with ladies!

Charles!

Daddy!

SEASIDE HOLIDAY – 1843
In which, safely back in England, the Dickens family visits the seaside

In the centre of a tiny bay our house stands: the sea rolling and dashing under the windows. In a bay window sits, from nine o'clock to one, a gentleman with rather long hair, who writes and grins as if he thought he were very funny indeed. His name is Boz. At one, he disappears and presently emerges from a bathing machine, and then may be seen a kind of salmon-coloured porpoise – splashing about in the ocean.

Dickens always rented the same house at Broadstairs. There is now a Dickens House Museum in the town.

MARTIN CHUZZLEWIT (1843 - 44) is a tale of greed and wickedness that takes its hero to America.

A rich old man employs a beautiful nurse but disinherits his grandson, Martin, an architecture student, for falling in love with her.

Martin then falls foul of his relative and tutor Mr Pecksniff, who, hoping to inherit money from Martin's grandfather himself, banishes the young man.

The book is stuffed with marvellous characters, including wicked Jonas Chuzzlewit and roguish, but doomed, Tig Montague.

Martin tries to make his fortune in America and, although swindled out of all his savings, manages to return home to a surprise happy ending.

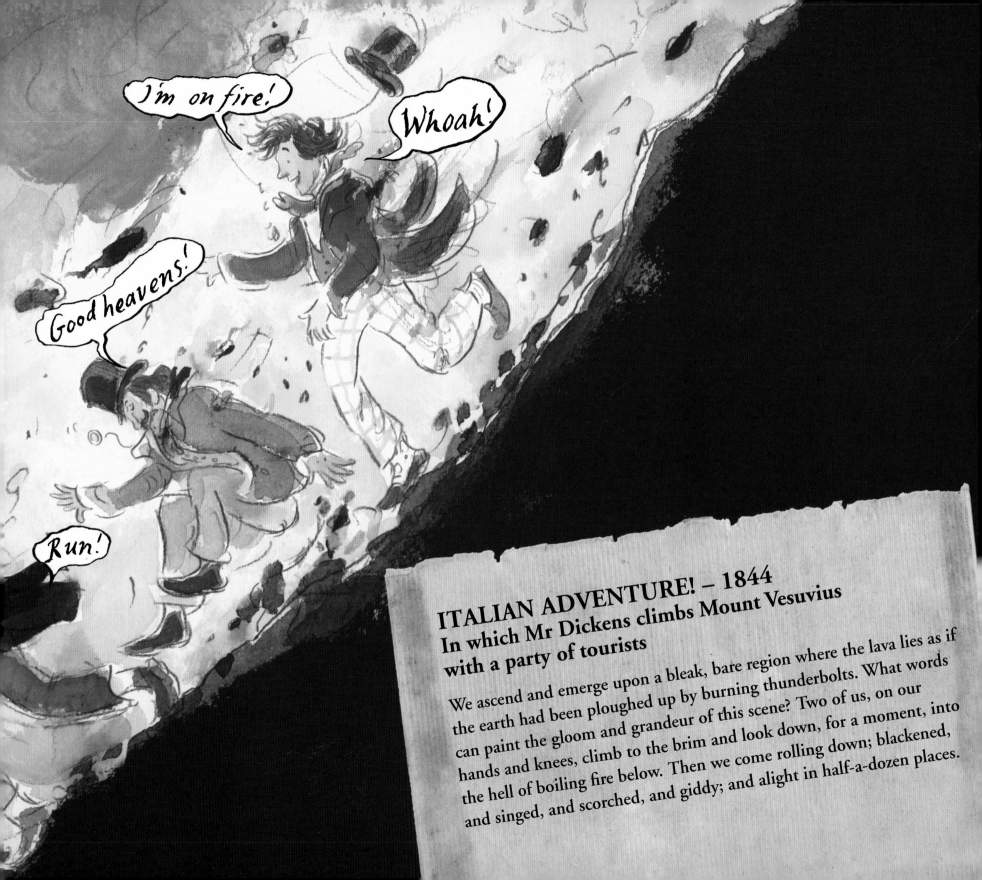

ITALIAN ADVENTURE! – 1844
In which Mr Dickens climbs Mount Vesuvius with a party of tourists

We ascend and emerge upon a bleak, bare region where the lava lies as if the earth had been ploughed up by burning thunderbolts. What words can paint the gloom and grandeur of this scene? Two of us, on our hands and knees, climb to the brim and look down, for a moment, into the hell of boiling fire below. Then we come rolling down; blackened, and singed, and scorched, and giddy; and alight in half-a-dozen places.

In 1844 Dickens bought an old stagecoach, large enough to take 12 people – his whole family and servants – on a journey through Italy. They lived there for many months and he wrote a book: *Pictures From Italy*. In 1846 and 1847 they also lived for periods of time in Switzerland and France, and saw many inspiring sights.

LITTLE DORRIT (1855-57), written some years after his travels, draws upon Dickens' years abroad and his father's time in prison.

Little Dorrit's eccentric father has been in a debtors' prison for so many years he has gone a little crazy.

Little Dorrit works hard for a rich lady and meets her son, Arthur, who has returned from China.

The rich lady has a secret and Arthur thinks it could be about Little Dorrit.

Thanks to friends, including Arthur, Mr Dorrit inherits a fortune and is able to leave prison.

The Dorrit family become snobbish to old friends like Arthur – all except for Little Dorrit.

Arthur tries to find out his mother's secret. He's sure it involves Little Dorrit. What can it be?

The Dorrits go away on holiday to Italy and meet a murderer...

Many more exciting things happen next. Read the book!

DAVID COPPERFIELD (1849-50) tells us much about Charles Dickens' own childhood.

David's father dies before he is born. His rich aunt, Betsy Trotwood, is so disappointed the baby is not a girl, she leaves.

David's mother remarries, but the stepfather is a bully and beats young David.

David bites his stepfather in self-defence and is sent to boarding school. Then his sick mother dies....

David's stepfather sacks Peggotty, his mum's friendly housekeeper, and sends David to work in a London factory.

This book is peppered with wonderful characters – many inspired by people Dickens knew and loved.

But it's not all sad. He lodges with Mr Micawber, a jolly man who becomes almost a father to David.

But when, like Dickens' own father, Mr Micawber is sent to a debtors' prison, David runs away…

He finds his aunt Betsy and she looks after him. He is renamed Trotwood.

Read the whole exciting story and meet brave 'Trot', sinister Uriah Heep and lovely Agnes.

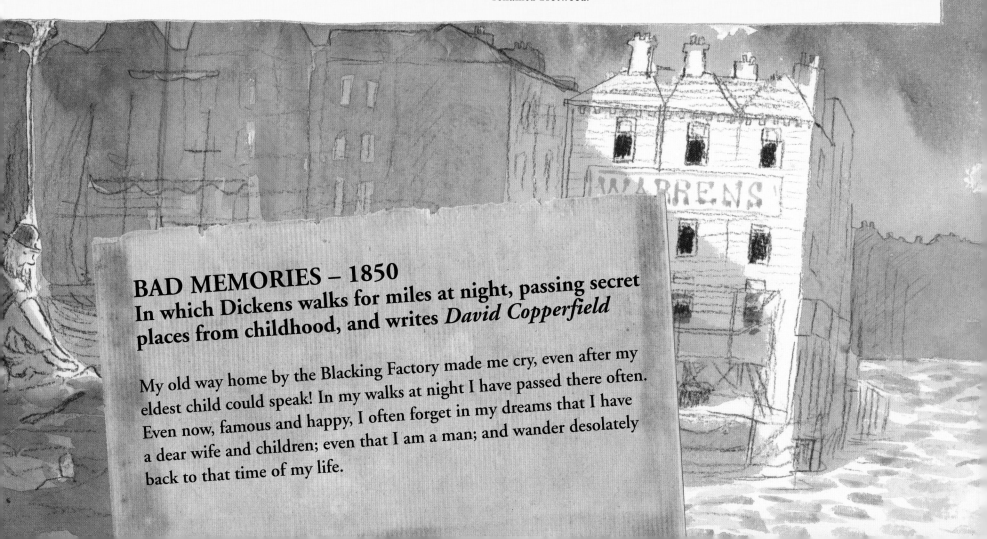

BAD MEMORIES – 1850
In which Dickens walks for miles at night, passing secret places from childhood, and writes *David Copperfield*

My old way home by the Blacking Factory made me cry, even after my eldest child could speak! In my walks at night I have passed there often. Even now, famous and happy, I often forget in my dreams that I have a dear wife and children; even that I am a man; and wander desolately back to that time of my life.

ON DUTY WITH INSPECTOR FIELD – 1851
In which our hero goes on patrol with Scotland Yard detectives to a thieves' rookery

How goes the night? The weather is dull and wet, and the street lamps are blurred, as if we saw them through tears. We stoop low, and creep down a flight of steps into a dark cellar full of very young men in various conditions of dirt and raggedness. Inspector Field's roving eye searches every corner as he talks. Every thief here cowers before him, like a schoolboy before his schoolmaster. All watch him, all laugh at his jokes. One pickpocket, especially, laughs with great enthusiasm. O what a jolly game it is, when Mr Field comes down – and don't want nobody!

Dickens' fascination for detectives inspired one of the first fictional police detectives: Inspector Bucket. The 'who-dunnit' was born!

BLEAK HOUSE (1852-53) concerns relatives squabbling to inherit property and a fortune – and a dark secret.

Generations of relatives argue in court about inheriting a fortune...

and the mysterious Lady Dedlock has a secret. . .

A clerk, Mr Guppy, loves a clever girl called Esther. Is she really an orphan?

There are two cousins, Richard and Ada, who fall in love....

A ruthless lawyer called Tulkinghorn is murdered.

Can Inspector Bucket solve the case and save the day?

A CHRISTMAS CAROL (1843) became everyone's favourite Christmas fairy tale.

Scrooge is a mean miser who works his poor clerk, Bob Cratchit, very hard. Bob has a large family.

One of his children, Tiny Tim, is disabled.

One Christmas Eve Scrooge is visited by ghosts – his old partner, Jacob Marley, and the ghost of Christmas Past, who reminds him of his lonely childhood.

The ghost of Christmas Present shows Scrooge the Cratchit family's meagre Christmas – but when the Ghost of Christmas Yet To Come shows the possible death of Tiny Tim, Scrooge is horrified.

He wakes up a new man, becoming kind and generous to everyone. Read this Christmas fairy tale yourself!

Dickens loved to read *A Christmas Carol* to his friends and family. This story helped to create the Victorian 'season of goodwill' as we enjoy it today, along with Christmas trees and carol singing.

CHRISTMAS WITH MR DICKENS – 1856
In which our hero invites family and friends to his home

I am looking at a merry company of children assembled round a Christmas tree. The tree towers high above their heads. It is brilliantly lighted by a multitude of little tapers; and everywhere sparkles and glitters with bright objects. There are rosy-cheeked dolls, fiddles and drums; paint-boxes and trinkets for the older girls. There is a smell of roasted chestnuts, for we are telling Winter Stories – Ghost Stories – round the Christmas fire.

It looks Magical

Boz suits a beard, Forster!

He does, Phiz, he does!

Scrooge was better than his word and to Tiny Tim, who did not die, he was a second father. And so, as Tiny Tim observed, "God Bless Us, Every One!"

ON TOUR – 1861
In which Mr Dickens performs at the King's Arms Hotel, Berwick upon Tweed

I write (in a gale of wind, with a high sea running), to let you know that we go on to Edinburgh at half-past-eight tomorrow morning. A most ridiculous room was designed for me in this odd, out-of-the-way place. An immense Corn Exchange… full of thundering echoes, with a little, lofty, crow's-nest of a stone gallery, breast high, deep in the wall, into which it was designed to put me! I said I would either read in a room attached to this house or not at all.

Dickens toured the country giving public readings. His surviving letters tell us much about these busy times.

Goodness me!

GREAT EXPECTATIONS (1860-61) is a story of love and hope that begins on the lonely, windswept marshes near a prison hulk.

The orphan Pip lives on the wild marshes with his cruel sister and her husband Joe, the blacksmith. Joe is Pip's only friend.

While alone at his parents' grave, Pip is terrified by an escaped convict. He fetches him food and a file to break his chains.

Pip is sent to play with a rich little girl, Estella. Her guardian, Miss Haversham, was jilted at the altar years ago, and still sits beside a mouldy feast, wearing her wedding dress.

Pip loves Estella but she just teases him cruelly. When older, Pip mysteriously inherits a fortune and moves to London.

Jaggers, the lawyer, won't tell him where the money comes from. Pip thinks it is from Miss Haversham.

But the truth is a shock! Dramatic chapters unfold revealing the truth about Magwitch, Miss Haversham... and Estella.

Dickens put all his emotions into his performances. An extract from *Oliver Twist*, called The Death of Nancy, would exhaust him.

TRAIN CRASH – 1865
In which our hero narrowly escapes death while travelling by steam train

I was in the only carriage that did not go over into the stream, and hung suspended in an apparently impossible manner. Two ladies were my fellow passengers: an old one, and a young one. The old lady cried out, "My God!" and the young lady said in a frantic way, "Let us join hands and die friends." I said to them thereupon: "You may be sure nothing worse can happen." I got out with great caution and stood upon the step. Looking down, I saw the bridge gone and nothing below me. . .

I left it here somewhere!

The Staplehurst rail crash killed 10 people. Dickens risked his life climbing back into the wreckage to rescue his latest episode of *Our Mutual Friend* for publication in his magazine All the Year Round.

Help!

All the Year Round had been published by Dickens since 1859, and included serials and short stories by himself and other authors. A year after the crash Dickens wrote a spine-chilling, railway ghost story called *The Signalman*.

LAST DAYS – 1870
In which the world-famous Charles Dickens visits Queen Victoria, goes to the zoo and begins *The Mystery of Edwin Drood*

It was at the Zoo, and my son and I were walking down the broad walk when we saw, a little distance away from us, a lady and gentleman coming towards us with a bright and pretty girl running ahead of them. Suddenly the little girl, catching sight of us, ran back to her mother, crying out delightedly, "Oh, Mummy! Mummy! It is Charles Dickens." I was strangely embarrassed; but, oh, so pleased, so truly delighted.

Queen Victoria had been to see some of Dickens' theatrical performances, and on 9th March, 1870, she invited him to Buckingham Palace. After the visit, Dickens sent her a set of his novels bound in red leather.

On 9th June, 1870, aged only 58, worn out by
his hectic life-style, and before he could complete
The Mystery of Edwin Drood, Charles Dickens died.
He is buried in Westminster Abbey, London.
His amazing stories have since become costume dramas,
films, TV series, animations, plays and musicals.
His books are read all over the world, making
Dickens one of the greatest writers of all time.

Glossary

Architect – someone who designs buildings

Blacking – boot polish

Debtors' prisons – there was no bank credit in those days and if you owed money you could be sent to prison until the debt was paid

Epidemic – an outbreak of infectious disease

Hard labour – a prison sentence of hard, back-breaking work

Industrial and Agricultural Revolutions – Ages of new invention and enterprise that brought about huge changes to society and to the sorts of work poor people had to do

Pay clerk – someone involved in calculating and giving out the workers' wages – for example, in a shipyard

Prison Hulks – floating prisons made from derelict ships

Rascality – an old word meaning trickery

Rat's Castle – a local den of orphans who had turned to crime

Scotland Yard – the offices of the new police detectives

Slums – the poorest, most overcrowded areas of a city

Tuberculosis – an infectious disease that affects the lungs

Vesuvius – a huge, dangerous Italian volcano

Workhouse – In those days there was no social security. The jobless poor, the homeless and the helpless were all sent to their local workhouse. Workhouses gave people food and shelter in return for unpaid work. Those in charge treated people badly; husbands and wives were separated and families split up. Old people often died of shame and loneliness once in the workhouse.

References and inspiration
The works of Charles Dickens
Letters by Charles Dickens, his friends and associates
The Life of Charles Dickens, John Forster
My Father As I Recall Him, Mamie Dickens
Memories of My Father, Henry Fielding Dickens
Dickens, Peter Ackroyd
Francis Cowe, historian, Berwick on Tweed
David Perdue's online Charles Dickens pages
The Dickens House Museum, Doughty Street, London
The Dickens House Museum, Broadstairs, Kent
Re-enactment of a Dickens reading by Pip Utton, Edinburgh Festival 2010
Miss Sheen, the author's English teacher at Greenhead School, Keighley 1974-78
Roddi and Karen at Berrydin Books, Berwick upon Tweed
The Charles Dickens' Birthplace Museum, Portsmouth

Works by Charles Dickens, mentioned in this book
A Dinner at Poplar Walk (1833)
Sketches by Boz (1833-36)
The Pickwick Papers (1836-37)
Oliver Twist (1837-38)
Nicholas Nickleby (1838-39)
The Old Curiosity Shop (1840-41)
A Christmas Carol (1843)
Martin Chuzzlewit (1843-44)
Pictures from Italy (1846)
David Copperfield (1849-50)
Bleak House (1852-53)
Little Dorrit (1855-57)
Great Expectations (1860-61)
Our Mutual Friend (1864-65)
The Signalman (1866)
The Mystery of Edwin Drood (1870)

Dickens' 'own words' used in the main text
Baby Dickens – adapted from *David Copperfield*
Happy Days – abridged from *Life of Charles Dickens* by John Forster
Moving to London – abridged from *The Uncommercial Traveller*
Lost! – abridged from *London Sketches*
Alone!– abridged from *London Sketches*
I Must Work! – abridged from *Life of Charles Dickens* by John Forster
My Father is Arrested! – abridged from *Life of Charles Dickens* by John Forster
School at Last! – abridged from *Our School*, Household Words
I am a Reporter – abridged from a speech to the Press Fund and quotes
   from John Forster
Love and Marriage – abridged from writing by Charles Dickens
Oliver! – adapted from *My Father As I Recall Him* by Mamie Dickens
Smike! – abridged from a letter written by Charles Dickens
Sailing for America – abridged from *American Notes*
America! – based on a letter to Frederick Dickens
Seaside Holiday – abridged from a letter quoted by John Forster
Italian Adventure! – abridged from *Pictures from Italy*
Bad Memories – adapted from *Life of Charles Dickens* by John Forster
On Duty with Inspector Field – abridged from *On Duty with Inspector Field*
Christmas with Mr Dickens – abridged from *A Christmas Tree*, Household Words
On Tour – abridged from a letter written by Charles Dickens
Train Crash – abridged from a letter written by Charles Dickens
Last Days – adapted from *Memories of My Father*, Henry Fielding Dickens